I0111392

Grace and Gravy
Devotionals for Your Journey
Charles E. Cravey

In His Steps Publishing

Copyright © 2025 by Charles Edward Cravey

All rights reserved.

No portion of this book may be reproduced in any form without written permission from the publisher or author, except as permitted by U.S. copyright law.

ISBN (paperback): 978-1-58535-098-8

ISBN (Kindle): 978-1-58535-099-5

Library of Congress Catalog Number: 2025915742

All scripture is taken from the King James Version of the Bible unless otherwise noted. Used by permission.

Cover design by Charles E. Cravey

Published in the United States of America

Published by In His Steps Publishing, Statesboro, Georgia.

Table of Contents

Preface

Devotionals for Your Journey

I selected this title after writing and publishing *Biscuits and Grace, a Chicken Soup for the Soul*-inspired book. Grace and Gravy will follow a similar path, featuring more stories filled with inspiration and hope.

Recently, my wife, Renee, inquired why many of my book titles focus on Grace. I explained to her that everything in the Bible revolves around Grace and deserves to be shared with the world.

It's a concept that resonates deeply with me, as it embodies the essence of unconditional love and forgiveness. Grace is the thread that weaves through our daily lives, offering us moments of reflection and growth. In *Grace and Gravy*, I aim to capture the richness of life's experiences, much like the warmth of a comforting meal shared with loved ones.

Each story is a testament to the power of faith and the beauty of finding hope in unexpected places. From tales of overcoming adversity to simple moments of joy, the book is a celebration of the human spirit. I hope readers will find solace and encouragement in these pages and perhaps see a reflection of their own journeys within these stories.

My goal is to remind everyone that, just like a satisfying meal, life is best savored with a generous helping of grace.

--Charles E. Cravey, July 2025

Introduction

In my upbringing, gravy was an essential part of numerous meals. After Mama prepared her legendary fried chicken, cubed steak, pork steak, or a variety of other meats, she would pour off most of the grease and then mix in a bit of flour and water until it thickened into a rich gravy. When served over rice, mashed potatoes, or warm biscuits, it felt like "heaven on earth" for us boys!

While growing up, these meals were more than just food; they were moments of connection and comfort. Around the table, we shared stories, laughter, and sometimes tears, all seasoned with Mama's signature gravy. It was as if each meal was a chapter in our family's story, binding us together with love and tradition.

As I reflect on those cherished times, I realize that gravy, much like grace, has a way of enhancing the ordinary, turning simple ingredients into something extraordinary. It reminds me of the small but significant acts of kindness and compassion that can transform our daily lives.

In *Grace and Gravy*, I hope to convey that same sense of warmth and belonging. Just as a good meal can nourish the body, grace can nourish the soul, offering healing and hope. Through the stories shared in this book, may you find your own moments of grace that fill your heart with gratitude and joy.

Each story is a gentle reminder that grace is always present, ready to uplift us even in the most mundane of circumstances. Whether it's through a kind word from a stranger, the unwavering support of a friend, or a quiet moment of introspection, grace can reveal itself in countless, unexpected ways.

As you journey through the pages of *Grace and Gravy*, I invite you to savor each narrative, allowing the lessons and reflections within to settle into your heart. Much like the way Mama's gravy enriched our family gatherings, may these stories enrich your own life, encouraging you to seek and cherish those moments of grace that often go unnoticed.

Let us embark on this journey together, embracing the beauty and strength found in grace, and discovering the profound impact it can have on our lives. May this book be a companion on your path, inspiring you to share your own stories of grace with those around you.

A popular quote about gravy is that it's "the glue that holds a meal together." Much like grace, it brings harmony to the diverse elements on our plate, enhancing and elevating each component. Just as gravy ties a meal into a cohesive experience, grace binds our lives, connecting moments of joy, sorrow, growth, and reflection into a meaningful journey.

1

"In the Beginning..."

Genesis 1:1

Grace was there in the beginning, before anything else. And of course, we know that God the Father, God the Son (Jesus), and God the Holy Spirit were all that existed at the time. We are not going to argue about science or theories concerning this; we'll keep it simple and to the point.

Grace, in its purest form, is the foundation upon which everything else was built. It was present at the dawn of creation, setting the stage for all that would follow. Just as God crafted the heavens and the earth, grace was the gentle force that permeated every act of creation, infusing it with love and purpose.

In those early moments, before the stars glittered in the sky and the oceans roared upon the shores, grace was the silent undercurrent, guiding the divine hands that shaped the universe. It was there when life first stirred, a testament to the beauty and potential that lay within every living thing.

As we reflect on this concept, it becomes clear that grace is not merely an abstract idea but a tangible presence that continues to influence our world today. It is the quiet strength that supports us through our challenges, the light that shines in times of darkness, and the peace that envelops us when we most need it.

Throughout the stories in *Grace and Gravy*, this theme of grace as an ever-present force in our lives will be explored and celebrated. From the miracles of everyday life to the extraordinary moments that take our breath away, grace is the common thread that ties it all together.

May we recognize and embrace grace in all its forms, allowing it to guide us, uplift us, and transform our lives as it has done since the very beginning.

Genesis 1:1 gives us the BEGINNING. No need to know exactly how God created or how many millions of years ago it occurred, just that **HE** created. In the grand tapestry of existence, the act of creation itself is a testament to the boundless grace that flows from the Divine. It's a reminder that the details of how the universe came into being, while fascinating, are secondary to the profound truth that it was brought forth by a loving Creator.

This foundational grace is what invites us to marvel at the world around us, to find joy in the beauty of a sunrise, and to seek meaning in the complexity of life. It's an invitation to trust in the process and to embrace the mystery with faith and humility.

As we journey through life, let us hold onto this understanding, knowing that grace is ever-present, just as it was at the beginning. It encourages us to live with gratitude, to extend kindness to

As we navigate the complexities of life, may we remain open to the boundless grace that envelops us, allowing it to illuminate our paths and inspire us to be vessels of love and light in the world.

One of the Greek philosophers once said about grace that it is "the unmerited favor of the gods, bestowed upon humanity as a testament to their benevolence." This ancient perspective highlights the timeless nature of grace, suggesting that it is a universal concept that transcends cultural and historical boundaries. The philosopher recognized grace as a gift that flows from a divine source, offering hope and renewal to all who receive it.

This idea resonates deeply with the essence of *Grace and Gravy*, as it reminds us that grace is not confined to any single tradition or belief system. It is a shared human experience that connects us across time and space, inviting us to embrace the kindness and compassion that grace inspires.

As we explore the stories within this book, let us remember that grace is a bridge that links us to one another, fostering understanding and empathy in a world often divided by differences. It is a reminder that, regardless of our backgrounds or beliefs, we are all recipients of this extraordinary gift, called to reflect its light in our interactions and relationships.

May we carry this ancient wisdom forward, allowing grace to guide our hearts and actions, and discovering the profound impact it can have on our lives and the lives of those around us.

So, "In the beginning . . ." resounds with authority. There is a complete universe wrapped up in that brief statement at the beginning of our study.

GRACE AND GRAVY IN OUR STORY:

At the heart of our story, "In the Beginning...", the essence of "Grace and Gravy" lies in the delicate balance between elegance and warmth, much like an exquisitely crafted meal that nourishes both body and soul. Grace is found in the gentle unfolding of each chapter, where characters navigate their lives with poise, even in the face of adversity. It is in the kindness and understanding they extend to one another, creating a tapestry of connections that bind them together.

Gravy, on the other hand, represents the richness and flavor of life, the small moments that add depth and satisfaction to the narrative. It is the laughter shared over a communal meal, the comfort of familiar traditions, and the joy found in unexpected places. Together, Grace and Gravy weave a story that is as comforting as it is inspiring, reminding us that even in the simplest beginnings, there is beauty and meaning waiting to be uncovered.

A PRAYER SEEKING GRACE:

Heavenly Father, we come before You with humble hearts, seeking the gentle touch of Your grace in our lives. We ask that You open our eyes to the beauty that surrounds us and fill our hearts with gratitude for the blessings we have received.

In moments of doubt, grant us the strength to trust in Your plan and the courage to follow where You lead. Help us to embrace the spirit of forgiveness, extending kindness to ourselves and others, just as You have shown us through Your boundless love.

May Your grace guide our steps, illuminating our path with wisdom and compassion. Let it be the anchor that holds us steady in the storms of life and the light that shines through our joy and sorrow.

As we journey through this world, may we become vessels of Your grace, sharing it freely with all we encounter. Teach us to see the divine spark within each person, fostering understanding and unity in our divided world.

We pray that Your grace will transform our lives, drawing us closer to You and to one another. May it inspire us to live with purpose, gratitude, and love, reflecting Your light in all that we do.

In Your holy name, we pray. Amen.

Grace Before the Dawn

Charles E. Cravey

Before the stars were scattered in the skies,

And oceans heaved with breath at God's command,

Grace lingered like a promise in His eyes.

A silent stream that carved the dreaming land.

In many traditions, God is portrayed as a guiding light, offering moral and ethical directions to humanity. This divine presence is often associated with qualities such as compassion, justice, and mercy, serving as a source of inspiration and strength for believers in their daily lives.

The relationship between humanity and God is another central theme explored in religious texts and teachings. For some, this relationship is deeply personal, characterized by prayer, meditation, and a sense of connection to something greater than oneself. For others, it is expressed through communal worship and shared rituals that bring people together in a celebration of faith and spirituality.

The concept of God invites us to explore profound questions about existence, purpose, and the nature of the universe. It challenges us to consider our place in the cosmos and to seek understanding and harmony in our interactions with the world around us. Whether viewed through the lens of religion, philosophy, or personal belief, the exploration of God remains a timeless journey that continues to inspire and captivate the human spirit.

The ancient philosophers have been quoted as saying that understanding the divine is akin to trying to comprehend the vastness of the universe itself—a task both daunting and endlessly fascinating. Figures like Plato and Aristotle pondered the nature of a supreme being, considering the divine as the ultimate form of goodness and the prime mover who set the cosmos in motion. Their reflections laid the groundwork for future theological and philosophical discussions, influencing countless generations.

In Eastern philosophies, such as those found in Hinduism and Buddhism, the concept of God takes on different nuances. Here, the divine may be seen as a cosmic consciousness or an ultimate reality that transcends human understanding. These traditions often emphasize the interconnectedness of all life and the pursuit of enlightenment as a means to grasp the divine essence within each being.

Throughout history, the quest to understand God has intertwined with the human experience in profound ways. Sacred texts, art, music, and literature all serve as mediums through which humanity seeks to express its relationship with the divine, each offering a unique perspective on this eternal mystery. As we continue to explore these ideas, we contribute to a rich tapestry of thought and belief that spans cultures and centuries, reminding us of the shared journey we all undertake in our search for meaning and truth.

Early church theologians have said that understanding God is like trying to capture the wind—a pursuit that requires faith, humility, and a recognition of our own limitations. Figures such as Augustine of Hippo and Thomas Aquinas sought to reconcile human reason with divine revelation, striving to articulate a coherent understanding of God's nature and attributes. Augustine spoke of God as an unchanging presence, intimately involved in the world yet beyond human comprehension, encouraging believers to seek a personal relationship with the divine through love and grace.

Aquinas, on the other hand, emphasized the harmony between faith and reason, proposing that human intellect, though limited, could glimpse the divine through careful study and reflection. His works, particularly the "Summa Theologica," explored complex theological questions, offering insights that have shaped Christian thought for centuries.

These early theologians laid the foundation for a rich tradition of inquiry, inviting believers to explore the mysteries of faith with both heart and mind. Their teachings continue to inspire those who seek to understand the divine, offering guidance and wisdom to navigate the complexities of life with a sense of purpose and hope. As we delve into their reflections, we are reminded of the timeless pursuit of understanding that connects us across generations, inviting us to engage with the eternal questions that define our existence.

To the average layperson, God symbolizes a source of hope, comfort, and guidance in the complexities of everyday life. This divine presence represents the ultimate assurance that, despite life's uncertainties and challenges, there is a greater plan or purpose at work. For many, God embodies the ideals of love, forgiveness, and redemption, providing a moral compass and a sense of peace that transcends worldly troubles.

Ultimately, "Grace and Gravy" reminds us that our story, intertwined with the divine, is one of beauty, purpose, and boundless potential.

PRAYER FOR THE LAYPERSON:

Oh God of the Universe, the wind beneath our thoughts and comprehension, grant us the wisdom to seek Your presence in the everyday moments of our lives. May we find peace in the simplicity of our surroundings and strength in the quiet whispers of our hearts. Help us to embrace Your love as a guiding light, illuminating our path through the trials and triumphs we encounter.

In our moments of doubt, remind us of Your unwavering presence, a gentle reminder that we are never alone. Inspire us to extend kindness and compassion to those around us, seeing Your reflection in every face we meet. May our actions reflect the grace and mercy You bestow upon us, enriching our world with harmony and understanding.

As we journey through the tapestry of life, may our hearts remain open to Your teachings and our spirits receptive to Your divine wisdom. Guide us to live each day with purpose, gratitude, and joy, ever mindful of the blessings You have bestowed upon us. In Your infinite love, may we find our true selves and the courage to pursue a life of meaning and fulfillment. Amen.

The Name That Spoke the Stars Awake

Charles E. Cravey

In whispered depth, before the voice was heard,

God lingered in the hush that cradled night.

His name the breath that formed the sacred word.

His gaze was the spark that birthed the morning light.

From lofty scrolls to fire-lit village songs,

The quest for Him was etched in every heart.

Though creeds divide and centuries stretch long,

His grace remains, unmoved by time or art.

To know this God—the vast, unknowable—

Is not to master, but to kneel and see

That He who flung the stars was merciful,

And walks among us still, both wild and free.

We speak His name with awe, not to impress—

But to remember: love is God's address.

3

"In the Beginning God CREATED..."

The Wonder and Marvel of Creation

"Created" and "creation" are the operative words in this section of our study. They signify not just an action, but a profound sense of purpose and intentionality. When we delve into the concept of creation, we're exploring the foundation of existence, a moment where potential becomes reality. This idea resonates across various cultures and philosophies, each offering its unique interpretation of how the universe and life came into being.

In many traditions, creation is seen as a divine act, a manifestation of cosmic will or divine love. It is often portrayed as a harmonious and ordered process, where chaos is transformed into structure, and voids are filled with life and meaning. This transformative power of creation highlights the themes of innovation, growth, and transformation that continue to inspire human creativity and exploration.

As we study "created" and "creation," we also reflect on our own capacity to create and shape our world. Whether through art, science, or everyday actions, we participate in this ongoing narrative of creation, contributing to the tapestry of life with our unique expressions and efforts. Thus, understanding creation is not just about looking back at origins but also about recognizing our role in the continuous unfolding of the universe.

In embracing this role, we become co-creators in our own right, crafting stories, innovations, and relationships that ripple through time. Each decision, no matter how small, adds a new thread to the intricate weave of existence. This perspective empowers us to approach life with a sense of wonder and responsibility, knowing that our actions have the potential to shape not just our own lives, but the world around us.

Moreover, the act of creation is inherently hopeful. It speaks to our ability to bring forth something new and beautiful, to imagine possibilities beyond the present, and to strive for a future that reflects our highest ideals. In this light, creativity becomes a bridge between the tangible and the intangible, the known and the unknown, and the present and the future.

As we navigate this journey, we are reminded that every challenge is an opportunity for creation, every problem a canvas for innovation. In this way, we honor the legacy of creation that has been passed down through generations while also forging new paths for those who will come after us.

Early philosophers viewed the Creation as a profound mystery, a subject of endless contemplation and debate. They pondered the origins of the universe with a sense of awe and curiosity, seeking to understand not only how it came into being but also why. For many, the act of creation was inextricably linked to the divine, a testament to the presence of a higher power orchestrating the cosmos with wisdom and intent.

In ancient Greece, thinkers like Plato and Aristotle offered differing views on creation. Plato envisioned a world crafted by a divine artisan, the Demiurge, who brought order to chaos using eternal forms as blueprints. Aristotle, on the other hand, introduced the concept of the "Unmoved Mover," a perfect being that set the universe in motion without itself being moved, emphasizing a more abstract, philosophical understanding.

Meanwhile, in Eastern philosophies, creation stories often emphasized cycles and the interconnectedness of all things. In Hinduism, the universe is born from the cosmic dance of Shiva, representing creation, preservation, and destruction in a perpetual cycle. Similarly, in Chinese philosophy, the balance of yin and yang symbolizes the dynamic forces that drive the universe's continuous creation and transformation.

These philosophical perspectives highlight humanity's enduring quest to comprehend the nature of existence and our place within it. They remind us that creation is not merely an event of the past but an ongoing process that invites us to explore, question, and contribute to the unfolding story of the world. Through this exploration, we gain insight into the essence of life itself, embracing both the known and the mysterious with an open heart and mind.

In the minds of our early church fathers, creation was often viewed as a divine act of love and wisdom, a reflection of God's infinite creativity and purpose. They perceived it as a moment when the divine intention manifested in the physical world, bringing forth beauty, order, and life from the void. Theologians like Augustine of Hippo pondered Creation as an expression of God's goodness, where everything created was inherently good and purposeful.

These early thinkers emphasized the idea that humanity, made in the image of God, is endowed with the capacity to reflect this divine creativity. This perspective encouraged believers to see themselves as stewards of Creation, tasked with nurturing and caring for the earth and all its inhabitants. The act of creation was seen not just as a historical event but as an ongoing partnership between the divine and humanity, where each person plays a role in the unfolding of God's plan.

For the early church fathers, understanding Creation also meant embracing a sense of wonder and gratitude. It was a call to recognize the sacred in the everyday, to find divinity in the world around us, and to live in a way that honors the Creator. This view inspired a legacy of theological reflection, art, and music that celebrated the mystery and majesty of Creation, inviting future generations to explore their own creative potential and spiritual journey.

Creation to the average layperson means many things, often rooted in personal experience and cultural context. For some, it may evoke images of the natural world, from majestic mountains and vast oceans to the intricate beauty of a blooming flower. It's the marvel of a night sky filled with stars, the gentle unfolding of seasons, and the mysterious dance of life in all its varied forms.

To others, creation might be more personal, tied to the acts of making and building. It can be found in the artist's brushstroke on a blank canvas, the writer's words weaving a story, or the engineer's blueprint coming to life. It's the satisfaction of baking a loaf of bread, planting a garden, or crafting a piece of furniture. In these acts, creation becomes a tangible expression of human ingenuity and imagination.

For many, creation is also deeply spiritual, a reflection of a greater narrative that transcends the individual. It can be a moment of awe and connection, where one feels part of something larger, a universe filled with purpose and meaning. Whether seen through the lens of religious faith or philosophical inquiry, creation speaks to the mystery of existence and invites us to ponder our place within it.

Creation for the average layperson is a reminder of the potential within us all to innovate, inspire, and bring something new into the world. It is a celebration of both the wonders we can observe and the wonders we can create, a testament to the enduring spirit of exploration and creativity that defines the human experience.

GRACE AND GRAVY IN OUR STORY:

When we explore the profound narrative of "In the beginning God CREATED," we can find the essence of both grace and gravy interwoven in the fabric of creation itself. Grace, in this context, is the unmerited favor and boundless love with which the universe was brought into existence. It is the divine generosity that infuses life with beauty and purpose, offering us a world rich in wonder and potential.

Gravy, on the other hand, can be seen as the abundance and richness that accompany creation. It's the overflowing bounty of nature—the lush landscapes, vibrant ecosystems, and the intricate balance of life. Just as gravy enhances a meal, the richness of creation adds depth and flavor to the human experience, inviting us to savor the gifts of existence.

Together, grace and gravy paint a picture of a world crafted with intention and care, inviting us to engage with it fully and appreciate the marvels that surround us. They remind us that creation is not just an event of the past but an ongoing story of generosity and abundance, encouraging us to live with gratitude and stewardship.

PRAYER FOR THE SEEKER:

Help me, Father, to understand the intricacies of your creation. Grant me the wisdom to see the beauty and purpose woven into every part of this world, from the grandest galaxies to the tiniest particles, each a testament to your infinite creativity and love. As I seek to comprehend these mysteries, open my heart to the wonder and awe that accompany true understanding.

Guide me to be a steward of your creation, nurturing it with care and respect, mindful of the delicate balance that sustains life. Encourage me to use my talents and insights to contribute positively, to innovate with compassion, and to inspire others through acts of kindness and creativity.

May my journey of discovery bring me closer to you, deepening my faith and enriching my spirit. Let this exploration of Creation serve as a bridge to a deeper connection with the divine, reminding me of my role in the ongoing story of this universe. Amen.

The Hands That Shaped the Morning Sky

Charles E. Cravey

He spoke, and light unraveled from the dark,

A tapestry of stars stitched into space.

Each whisper left creation with a mark,

A cradle formed by gravity and grace.

Mountains rose like prayers from oceans deep,

Fields unfolded in fragrant harmony.

The sparrow stirred; the lion woke from sleep—

All life is designed with sacred symmetry.

Yet more than form, He poured His heart inside:

The breath of love, the warmth of art divine.

So, we, His echoes, labor side by side—

To shape, to heal, to build, to intertwine.

For every dawn we craft, His voice remains:

In us, the spark of Eden still sustains.

4

"In the Beginning God Created the Heavens and the Earth"

The Earth was a blank canvas, a vast expanse of potential and wonder waiting to be shaped and filled with life. Light and darkness were separated, and day and night emerged in harmonious rhythm. The skies were painted with radiant stars, each one a beacon of mystery and possibility. The seas were teeming with life, vibrant and diverse, as creatures of all shapes and sizes danced through the waters. Lush landscapes formed, where flora and fauna flourished, creating a tapestry of life that was both intricate and breathtaking.

Amidst this burgeoning world, humanity was crafted with care and purpose. Gifted with curiosity and creativity, people were entrusted with the stewardship of this magnificent creation. They marveled at the beauty around them, inspired to explore, learn, and grow in harmony with the world they inhabited. As time unfolded, stories and cultures blossomed, each adding to the rich tapestry of human existence, filled with tales of triumph, challenge, and the enduring spirit of discovery.

Ancient philosophers viewed the creation of the heavens and earth in this fashion: a grand symphony orchestrated by divine hands, where each element played a crucial role in the cosmic dance of existence. They saw the stars as celestial guides, their light a reminder of eternity and the infinite possibilities of the universe. The earth, in their eyes, was a nurturing mother, offering sustenance and shelter, a sacred ground where humanity could thrive and find purpose.

These thinkers pondered the mysteries of the cosmos, contemplating the intricate balance of nature and the unseen forces that governed it. They believed that the physical world was imbued with spiritual significance, each element a reflection of a higher order and wisdom. The beauty and complexity of creation inspired them to seek knowledge and understanding, to question and explore the nature of reality and the divine.

In their teachings, they emphasized the interconnectedness of all things, urging people to live in harmony with the world and each other. They spoke of the importance of reverence and gratitude, of recognizing the sacredness in every living thing, and of the responsibility to protect and cherish the earth and its inhabitants. Through their insights, they laid the foundation for a deeper appreciation of the world and our place within it, encouraging future generations to continue the quest for wisdom and enlightenment.

Our early church fathers viewed the creation of "the heavens and the earth" in this fashion: a divine masterpiece, crafted with intentionality and purpose. They saw the universe as a testament to the Creator's boundless wisdom and love, where every element, from the tiniest grain of sand to the vast expanse of the sky, held a sacred significance. For them, the heavens were not merely a physical realm but a spiritual one, a place where the divine presence could be felt and contemplated.

The earth, with its rich diversity and beauty, was seen as a gift to humanity, a place of stewardship and responsibility. The church fathers taught that humanity was entrusted with the care of this world, to nurture and protect it as a reflection of divine grace. They emphasized living in accordance with divine principles and fostering a sense of community and compassion among all people.

Through their teachings, they encouraged a life of prayer and reflection, urging individuals to seek a deeper connection with the Creator and the created world. They believed that by understanding the divine order in creation, one could gain insight into the nature of God and the purpose of life. This understanding was seen as a path to spiritual enlightenment and fulfillment, a journey of discovering the divine within and all around.

Our contemporary layperson views this concept as an invitation to wonder and a call to action. In a world increasingly driven by technology and rapid change, the creation narrative resonates as a reminder of the profound beauty and mystery that surrounds us. For many, it underscores the importance of mindful living, where appreciation for the natural world and its delicate balance becomes paramount.

Today, people find themselves drawn to the idea of living sustainably, recognizing the need to protect our planet for future generations. This perspective encourages a harmonious existence with nature, where every action is considered in light of its impact on the environment. The creation story inspires individuals to cultivate a sense of stewardship, urging them to contribute positively to the world around them.

Moreover, the modern layperson often interprets the creation as a metaphor for personal growth and transformation. Just as the earth was shaped from chaos into order, individuals see their own lives as a journey of becoming, continually evolving in understanding and purpose. This narrative encourages introspection and the pursuit of knowledge, as people seek to align their lives with values that honor both themselves and the broader community.

The contemporary view transforms the creation story into a living tapestry of inspiration, one that calls for both awe and active engagement with the world. It serves as a gentle nudge to look beyond the mundane, to recognize the sacred in everyday life, and to embrace the interconnectedness of all things with gratitude and responsibility.

GRACE AND GRAVY IN OUR STORY:

Let's explore the profound beauty and harmony in this age-old narrative. The "grace" can be seen in the act of creation itself—a divine gesture of bringing forth existence from nothingness, a testament to boundless love and generosity. The universe, intricately crafted, reflects a harmonious order and endless possibilities, inviting us to marvel at its complexity and elegance.

The "gravy," on the other hand, might be considered as the richness and abundance that flow from this creation. It is the myriads of life forms, the vibrant colors of a sunset, the rhythmic lapping of ocean waves, and the whispering of the wind through trees. These elements add flavor and depth to our world, enhancing our experiences and connecting us to the divine narrative.

Together, grace and gravy create a tapestry of existence that is both awe-inspiring and humbling, reminding us of our place within this grand cosmos and inviting us to live with gratitude and wonder.

PRAYER FOR UNDERSTANDING:

Lord, show me your ways, teach me your paths, and guide me in your truth. Grant me the wisdom to discern your presence in the world around me and the humility to learn from all that you have created. Open my heart to the beauty of your creation and the lessons it holds, so that I may walk in harmony with your divine purpose.

Help me to embrace each day with gratitude and curiosity, seeking to understand the mysteries of your universe and my place within it. May I be a steward of your earth, caring for it with love and respect, and may my actions reflect your compassion and grace. In my journey towards knowledge and enlightenment, let your light be my guide, illuminating the path before me and inspiring me to live with integrity and joy.

Amen.

When Grace Was Etched in Earth and Sky

Charles E. Cravey

He traced the stars with hands both wise and kind.

Each gleam a thought, each orbit spun with care.

The seas obeyed the whisper of His mind,

And forests bloomed beneath His silent prayer.

The earth received His gift of light and breath,

Its rhythms tuned to mercy's gentle sway.

From chaos' edge to life's triumphant depth,

Creation sang what words could not convey.

Philosophers once called the world a song,

And saints beheld its beauty as a scroll.

Now laymen walk with reverence all along—

In tree and tide, they find a speaking soul.

So let us live as stewards of His grace,

And see His glory in this sacred place.

5

"In the Beginning God Created Me..."

Personal Creation and Identity in Grace

I was not born in a blaze of glory, nor summoned by the call of trumpets. I entered this world quietly, swaddled in mystery and mercy. But make no mistake—my arrival was not incidental. I am here because Grace willed it.

Before I was ever cradled in my mother's arms or kissed by the Georgia sun, the voice that split the firmament also whispered my name. The same God who slung stars across the heavens and molded mountains into majesty reached into the dust and shaped me—not just as a body, but as a soul. And He did so with the same gentleness that stirs the gravy pot at dawn, slow and deliberate, seasoned with love.

Psalm 139 tells us that we were knit together in the womb—intricately, purposefully, stitch by sacred stitch. That kind of craftsmanship doesn't happen by accident. It's a divine embroidery of personality, memory, and calling. My quirks, my shortcomings, my hunger for grace—they are all part of this divine pattern.

Theologians have written volumes on the imago Dei—the image of God stamped upon every human heart. I won't pretend to explain it all. But I believe it's in the way I hold a child's hand when they're frightened. Or the way my heart swells at the scent of biscuits baking on a Saturday morning. It's not grandeur—it's presence. It's not perfection—it's grace poured into clay.

Mama used to say, "You're sugar and salt, baby. Sweetness with a little bite." Maybe that's what creation looks like in real-time: not flawless people, but flawed souls loved perfectly.

I was made to reflect Him. Not in brilliance, but in belonging.

And so, with each breath I take, I try to live like someone who was created with intention. I try to speak grace as if it were the language of my lungs. I try to remember that before I ever lifted a prayer, God had already whispered, "You are Mine."

Scripture Reflection:

"I praise You because I am fearfully and wonderfully made; Your works are wonderful; I know that full well." —Psalm 139:14

A Prayer of Belonging:

Creator of galaxies and granaries,
You did not overlook me.
You saw me when only dust remembered my name,
And You called me beloved.

Help me live like someone You crafted—

With grace in my gait and mercy on my tongue.

May I never forget that I am the work of Your hands,

And may I treat others as Your handiwork too.

Amen.

Mercy's Gentle Hands Made me

Charles E. Cravey

Before I spoke a word or drew a breath,

His voice had written wonder in my frame.

He shaped my soul with love that mocked all death,

And signed my life with mercy's hidden name.

No accident, no fleeting flash of chance—

But artistry divinely set in place.

Each step ordained, each glance a sacred dance,

Each flaw is embraced within the arms of grace.

I am His work—not perfect but designed.

No trait forgotten, nothing left unspun.

He wove my past with future still aligned,

And blessed the road before it had begun.

So, I shall live as one whom God has known—

A vessel poured from heaven's heart alone.

6

"In the Beginning God Called..."

The Gentle Call of Purpose and Presence

It wasn't thunder. It wasn't fire falling from heaven. It wasn't a prophet's robe draped over my shoulders or a blinding light on the road.

No, when God called me, it came like the whisper of biscuits baking in the kitchen—slow, subtle, sweet.

I was just a boy when I first felt it. Not in church, but in Mama's garden. She was humming a hymn I didn't know, pulling weeds like she was praying. "You hear that?" she asked, pointing at the breeze. "That's God telling the earth what time it is." I didn't understand, but something stirred. It was warmth without fire, invitation without demand.

Calling has always worked that way with me. Not a single moment—but a series of them. A knock at a screen door. A stranger who needed a ride. A verse that landed too perfectly in my lap. A hand on my shoulder when I was too tired to stand.

God calls not just the preacher, not just the prophet. He calls the cook, the greeter, and the encourager. He calls the quiet ones who show up early and stay late. The ones who set the table for the soul.

Mama said hospitality was holiness you could smell. I think that's where my calling began. Not in a pulpit, but in a kitchen. Not in fire, but flour.

Even now, I feel it when I stir gravy with grandchildren watching. When I pray over a table filled with mismatched plates and second helpings. When I listen to someone's broken story and whisper, "You're still loved."

God's call is not always to do something grand. Sometimes, it's just to be—present, gentle, faithful.

And in those moments, I answer not with eloquence, but with open hands.

Scripture Reflection:

"In quietness and trust is your strength."
Isaiah 30:15

A Prayer for Clarity in Calling:

Speak, Lord—not in wind or quake,
But in the quiet spaces of my soul.
Let me hear Your voice in bread baking,

In tears, shared,

In laughter between generations.

May I never miss the whisper

Because I was waiting on the shout.

Amen.

The Whisper That Woke My Soul

Charles E. Cravey

Not in the fire, nor tempests bold and loud,

But in the stillness where the silence grew,

He found my heart beneath the worldly crowd,

And touched it with a purpose faint but true.

It came not dressed in titles or acclaim,

No flaming sword, no lightning in the skies.

Just one soft word that carried love and name,

A beckoning I could not analyze.

He called me through the laughter of the small,

Through hands that fed and tears the hurting cried.

Not once—but daily does His mercy call,

And walks with me where others might deride.

I answer not with flawless, holy tone—

But with a life that listens, not alone.

7

"In the Beginning God Called Them..."

Then hey were fishermen and tax collectors. Tentmakers and weepers. Sons and daughters. The ones with strong backs and soft hearts. The ones whose names were unknown but whose faith changed history.

God never worked alone. From Eden's garden to Galilee's shores, He called people *together*.

I've seen it with my own eyes. A casserole taken to a widow's home. A church van packed tight with laughter and youth group chaos. A table where grace multiplies in the passing of biscuits and second chances. When God calls *them*, He calls *us*. His plan was never about solitary saints—it was always about sacred togetherness.

Mama used to say, "Even gravy needs something to cling to." That's the heart of community. We hold each other. We season each other. We soak up grace together.

There were moments in my life when I wanted to walk alone—to prove my strength, to guard my heart. But grace wouldn't allow it. Grace always led me back to *them*. The people I pray with. The people who hug without asking questions. The people who show up with folding chairs and a word of hope.

It's the shared burden that becomes a shared blessing. The grief halved and the joy doubled. That's the math of mercy.

We were not created to be heroes. We were created to be humble parts of holy people. Called, not for greatness, but for gracefulness.

Scripture Reflection:

"For where two or three are gathered in My name, there am I with them."

—Matthew 18:20

A Prayer for Community Calling:

Gather us, God—not just in body, but in heart.

Help us hear Your voice in conversations, in casseroles, and in kindness exchanged.

Call us to walk together, to weep together, to believe together.

Amen.

The Table Where We All Belong

Charles E. Cravey

We were not made for solitary grace,

But formed for fellowship that sings and stays.

He set us round the table, face to face,

And filled the room with love's unfolding rays.

One pours the tea, one brings the bread to break,

Another lifts a hymn through quiet tears.

Each hand becomes a healing for the ache,

Each word restores the soul that sorrow sears.

He calls not just the strong, but those who bend—

Who lean on grace and sit where mercy grows.

In every stranger waits a future friend,

And every burden shared becomes a rose.

So, pass the biscuits, offer up a prayer—

God's call was never meant for one but shared.

8

"In the Beginning God Sustained..."

Where Strength Simmered, Grace Stayed Warm

N ot just creation. Not just calling. Sustaining.

It's one thing to be made and summoned—but it's another to be kept. Held. Fed. Rested. He didn't drop us in the garden and disappear. He remained in the dew, the firelight, and the stillness. And He remains still.

I've felt His sustaining hand in places where my strength had run dry. In grief, when the seat at the table was suddenly empty. In uncertainty, when plans crumbled and prayer felt like whispering into the wind. In weariness, when the duties of service wore grooves into my soul. In all those places, He didn't just remind me I was called—He reminded me I was *carried*.

Sometimes He sustains through silence. Through the quiet clink of forks on china. Through hugs exchanged in church foyers. Through sunlit porch swings and porch prayers. Grace doesn't always shout—it often simmers.

Mama used to say, "The secret to good gravy is patience and low heat." That's how He keeps me. Not through quick fixes but through slow-simmering presence. A kind of holy endurance.

I've seen it in the lives of others, too. Saints who never preached a sermon but showed up every day, holding grief with dignity and faith. Folks who fed others with food and with peace. The ones who prayed in hospital rooms and parking lots and pews worn smooth by generations. That's sustaining grace.

When God sustains, He doesn't erase hardship—He infuses it with meaning. He stirs comfort into sorrow, wisdom into weakness, and joy into waiting.

And that's the kind of grace you don't forget.

Scripture Reflection:

"My grace is sufficient for you, for My power is made perfect in weakness."
2 Corinthians 12:9

A Prayer for Endurance:

God who remains, when I falter, don't let me fall.
When I tire, don't let me forget that You are the One who fed the Israelites
And still feed me—day by day.

Give me a grace that endures, not the kind that flashes,
But the kind that holds me steady until the morning breaks again.

Amen.

The Strength Beneath My Quiet Days

Charles E. Cravey

He does not lift me only when I rise,
But it holds me fast in moments I retreat.
His mercy hums beneath my weary sighs,
And places hope within my aching feet.

Not daily triumph, not applause or cheer,
But steady grace that walks where no one sees.
The whispered word, "You're not alone, I'm near,"
Restores my soul in sacred subtleties.

Through morning coffee, through the quiet chore,
Through sighs exchanged on rocking porch-bound seats—
His faithfulness becomes what I adore,
The song that echoes in life's small repeats.

So let me live sustained, not for acclaim,
But held by grace that knows my truest name.

9

"In the Beginning God Restored..."

When Grace Took Me Back to the Table

B efore we ever wandered, Grace had already packed a lunch.

Because the truth is—we drift. We forget. We lose heart. We chase the world's noise and miss the Spirit's whisper. And yet, God waits. Not with arms folded, but with arms wide.

Restoration is not a guilt trip—it's a homecoming. I've known that kind of grace. I've felt it in the church pew I slid back into after a season of questioning. I've tasted it in sweet tea offered by someone who didn't need an apology to forgive me. I've heard it in the sound of hymnals rustling on a Sunday that should have been ordinary but wasn't.

Mama taught me that no matter how long the biscuits had sat, the gravy could still warm them back to life. That's restoration.

God doesn't just call the sinner—He restores the saint. He takes what's broken and gently re-forms it. Not like a craftsman fixing a vase, but like a gardener coaxing green from a frostbitten root.

Sometimes He restores through community. Sometimes through solitude. Sometimes through silence. But it always feels like grace taking us by the hand and leading us back to the table.

The same God who created me, who called me, who sustained me—is also the One who restores me. Again and again. Every time I forget. Every time I fall short. Every time I whisper, "Can I come home?"

He answers, "I never left."

Scripture Reflection:

"He restores my soul. He leads me in paths of righteousness for His name's sake."
Psalm 23:3

A Prayer for Restoration:

Restorer of broken roads,

Guide me back—not with guilt,

But with grace.

Let me find You in the quiet,

In the kindness,

In the casserole offered when I didn't deserve it.

Patch my heart with mercy,

And paint my spirit with hope once more.

Amen.

The Table Was Set Before I Knocked

Charles E. Cravey

I wandered far from where the feast was spread,
Through doubts and days where silence held its reign.
Yet grace prepared a path where I was led,
A table waiting, free from fear or stain.

No harsh rebuke, no ledger of regret—
Just warmth that wrapped around my weary frame.
The scent of welcome, kindness kindly met,
The whisper of forgiveness not named shame.

He found me not by map or measured chart,
But through the ache that pulled me home again.
Restored, renewed, He mended every part
And let me rest where healing could begin.

So now I live not fearing fall or flight—
For grace restores me, even in the night.

10

"In the Beginning God Provided..."

When Grace Came with Open Hands

G race rarely comes empty-handed.

From Eden's bounty to Elijah's ravens to Mama's biscuits spread with more love than butter—God has always been a provider. Not just of food or shelter, but of what our souls didn't know they hungered for.

I've seen Him provide in ways no budget could predict. A handshake that turned into a job. A casserole left on the porch after surgery. A verse tucked into a birthday card. It's often the kind of provision the world overlooks—but heaven calls it miraculous.

Mama said, "When the pantry gets low, that's when heaven opens up." She was never worried—because she knew provision came in people, not just packages. She taught me that sometimes *we* are the provision someone prayed for. A word. A presence. A hand steadying the pot.

God's provision isn't just survival—it's kindness. It's the second serving. The smile held just long enough. The silence that listens. It's the grace that arrives just when you thought you had to give up.

He provides peace when the storm won't stop. He provides purpose when direction feels lost. He provides enough—not always in surplus, but always in sufficiency.

I've come to believe that grace wears an apron. That it arrives quietly. That it never forgets where it's needed most.

Scripture Reflection:

"And my God will supply every need of yours according to His riches in glory in Christ Jesus."
—Philippians 4:19

A Prayer for Provision:

God of overflowing cupboards,

Give me eyes to see

The miracles in small things:

The extra biscuit,

The extra moment,

The extra mercy.

And make me a provider of grace—

Not just in things,

But in tenderness and truth.

Amen.

Grace in the Hands That Always Give

Charles E. Cravey

He saw my need before I knew to pray,
And sent the answer wrapped in quiet care.
Not thunder's roar, but mercy's gentle way,
A kindness placed like sunlight in the air.

The loaf was whole, the cup was never dry,
Though wants may shift and riches ebb and flow.
He met me with provision from on high,
In laughter shared and blessings whispered low.

No grand parade, no chariot of gold,
Just steady love in moments small and true.
A hand that feeds, a promise that will hold,
A daily grace that makes each morning new.

So let me live in trust—not doubt or fear—
For He who gives is always near.

11

"In the Beginning God Was With Me..."

When Grace Sat Beside Me at the Porch Swing

P resence is a kind of provision. It doesn't fix everything—it simply refuses to leave.

God was with me in the quiet. In the hum of cicadas. In the faded pages of my childhood Bible. In the sorrow that couldn't be spoken aloud and the joy that didn't need words.

I remember sitting on the porch swing after a long day, legs sore, heart tender. Mama came out with two glasses of sweet tea and nothing to say. She didn't need to. Her presence said everything: *I'm here.* I've come to know that's how God moves too.

He isn't only found in the sanctuary but also in screen doors and supper tables. He doesn't always preach—sometimes He just listens. And that listening is love.

Sometimes I've mistaken His silence for absence. But silence can be holy. It's not the absence of sound—it's the fullness of stillness. That's where grace rests.

God walks alongside us. Through grief, through labor, through boredom even. He's present in the waiting. Present in the rising. Present when faith feels thin and hope feels far.

I've learned that divine presence is the softest miracle. Not always grand. But always good.

Scripture Reflection:

"Fear not, for I am with you; be not dismayed, for I am your God."

—Isaiah 41:10

A Prayer for His Nearness:

God who stays,
Thank You for not needing a stage
to be seen.

Thank You for speaking in quiet
and staying in silence.

Teach me to recognize Your nearness—
In the laughter of children,
In the ache of loss,
In the stillness of my spirit
when all else is loud.

Amen.

The Presence That Asked Nothing in Return

Charles E. Cravey

No flash of light, no trumpet in the air,
Just whispered warmth beside my breaking ground.
He sat with me in sorrow, soft and fair,
And spoke no words, yet all my peace was found.

The stars did not announce His gentle stay,
No choir sang, and no preacher gave a sign.
But in that pause, my heart began to pray,
And I could feel His silence intertwine.

He did not ask for strength I couldn't give—
He simply stayed and let me breathe again.
And in His stillness, I relearned to live,
To rise each day beneath His calm Amen.

So let me be as He—so softly near,
A grace that stays, a love that casts out fear.

12

"In the Beginning God Loved..."

Where Grace First Found Its Voice

Before the earth rotated. Before mountains took shape or rivers carved paths. Before prophets, psalms, and sacraments—God loved.

Love was the seed, grace was the bloom.

I've come to understand that everything begins not with action, but with affection. God didn't just create out of ability—He created out of love. We are not divine experiments—we are beloved echoes.

Mama once said, "You know it's real love when someone stays past suppertime." That's how God loves. Unhurried, unshaken. Not just in moments of holiness, but in our mess, our wandering, our hesitation. He stays.

His love isn't earned—it's offered. Freely, like the gravy pot that never quite runs dry. I've felt it in laughter that interrupts grief. In memories that ache and heal at the same time. In unexpected forgiveness. In second chances—sometimes third and fourth.

This love doesn't conform to logic. It bends toward mercy. It stoops to wash feet. It walks dusty roads and welcomes prodigals with casseroles.

Everything—calling, restoration, presence—is only possible because love was first.

So, I live, not just sustained or summoned. I live loved.

Scripture Reflection:

"We love because He first loved us."
—1 John 4:19

A Prayer of Receiving:

God of first affection,

Teach me to live

Not just as a servant,

Not just as a seeker—

But as someone loved.

Let love be my root,

Grace my branch,

And kindness, my fruit.

Amen.

Love Was the First Word

Charles E. Cravey

Before the breath, before the spark and flame,
Love spoke the cosmos into quiet spin.
It carved my soul and softly wrote my name,
Not out of duty—but from joy within.

It holds me when I doubt what faith should mean,
And lifts me when my pride begins to fall.
Love finds me where my fear has grown unclean,
Then paints my shame with mercy over all.

No rule compelled it, no command decreed—
It simply bloomed, the way that roses do.
A grace so fierce, it meets my deepest need,
And stays when all the world forgets what's true.

So let me live as one the Lord adores,
A soul created by love's open doors.

13

"In the Beginning God Changed Me...

When Grace Rearranged the Furniture of My Soul

C hange is never easy. But grace doesn't bulldoze—it reno-
vates.

It doesn't demand overnight perfection. It works like Mama
tidying the front room—patiently, one corner at a time. Moving
furniture not for fashion, but for comfort. Rearranging what
already exists so it better welcomes what's to come.

I used to think change was all on me. That I had to fix myself to earn approval. But I've come to know that grace *gets to work* long before I do. It rearranges my priorities. It shifts my understanding. It clears out bitterness I didn't know had settled like dust in the corners.

Mama once said, "God don't mind using the same furniture—He just wants it set right." That's the gospel truth.

Grace changes us, not always in flashes, but in movements. It turns pride into gentleness. It turns judgment into listening. It turns routine into reverence. And it does so without asking for performance—just willingness.

God didn't change me to make me acceptable. He changed me because He already called me beloved. That truth makes all the difference.

The work is ongoing. Sometimes grace sweeps in like a fresh breeze. Other times, it's the gentle nudge to get up and try again.

And each time I let it, I find that grace has left things more holy than before.

Scripture Reflection:

"If anyone is in Christ, he is a new creation. The old has passed away; behold, the new has come."
—2 Corinthians 5:17

A Prayer for Transformation

God of slow renovations,
Change me in ways I won't even notice—
Until I respond to others with gentleness,
Until joy returns without fanfare,
Until I look back and say,
"I'm not who I was, thanks to grace."

Amen.

The Rearranging I Didn't Expect

Charles E. Cravey

He came not crashing through my stubborn walls,
But quietly, as light through morning lace.
He moved my heart where mercy softly calls,
And filled each space with newly borrowed grace.

He didn't change me out of need or wrath—
But love that saw what I could yet become.
He swept away my shame from hidden path,
And tuned my soul to grace's humble drum.

No spotlight shown, no echoing decree—
Just one small shift that turned despair to song.
He rearranged the soul inside of me,
So I could learn where faithful hearts belong.

Now I am changed—not finished, but restored,
A life reset by grace, not by reward.

14

"In the Beginning God Prepared..."

Where Grace Made Room Before I Knocked

G race is not reactive—it's anticipatory.

Before I ever faced a storm, He prepared a shelter. Before I spoke a prayer, He was listening. Before I knew I'd need strength, He had already planted it in someone near me—ready to share.

Mama used to say, "The Lord doesn't just answer prayers—He preps the kitchen before you get hungry." And Lord, have I seen it. A call from a friend I hadn't thought about in years. A verse appearing like a whisper in my memory. A door opening that I never knew I'd need to walk through.

Preparation is the quiet miracle. It's God laying out the silverware while I'm still wondering what we'll have for dinner.

Sometimes He prepares through people—those who carry grace in their gait. Sometimes through timing—when things come together so gently you know it wasn't coincidence. And sometimes through places—rooms that feel sacred though they've never held a sermon.

God's preparation isn't always flashy. It's a casserole warming in the oven while the house is still quiet. It's grace getting ready for the moment I didn't know was coming.

And that's what makes me trust Him—not just for what I see, but for what He's already stirred into motion.

Scripture Reflection:

"You prepare a table before me in the presence of my enemies..."
—Psalm 23:5

A Prayer for Preparedness:

God, who sets the table in advance,

Let me walk into the rooms You've readied—

Without fear,

Without trying to rearrange what You've placed.

Help me trust the timing,

The tools,

The tenderness You've already assigned to meet me there.

Amen.

The Place Was Set Before I Arrived

Charles E. Cravey

The path I walked was not unknown to grace.
Its stones were smoothed by mercy long before.
He carved a place, a quiet sacred space,
And left the light on through love's open door.

Before I knocked, the biscuits had been baked.
The chairs arranged, the teacups gently placed.
My doubts, though loud, were quietly unshaked
By peace prepared and tenderness embraced.

I did not earn the welcome that I found,
I simply came—and Grace was not surprised.
The table smiled without a single sound.
And I sat down where hope had been disguised.

So now I live with peace the world can't steal—
For He prepares before I even kneel.

15

"In the Beginning God Remained..."

Where Grace Waited Beside My Wandering Heart

Grace is not in a hurry. That's the first miracle.

The second is this: grace remains. Through every detour, doubt, and delay—it stays. It doesn't storm out when we forget scripture or skip prayer or wander toward lesser things. It pulls up a chair, folds its hands, and waits.

I've known what it is to be fickle. To feel like a flickering flame of faith one day, and a cold ember the next. But God? He remained. In the porch swing, in the prayer I couldn't form, in the silence that held me like a quilt stitched by mercy.

Mama once told me, "The people who matter don't leave when you mess up. They stay 'til the biscuits cool and you remember who you are." That's how I've come to recognize grace—it doesn't rush my repentance or demand spiritual excellence. It waits with me until I remember love.

Sometimes, we mistake movement for holiness. But grace shows us that presence is more powerful than progress. That remaining is its own kind of miracle.

God stayed in Eden after the fall. He stayed in the wilderness with wanderers. He stays in churches with creaky pews and in kitchens with peeling linoleum. He remains not just because He's faithful—but because He's in love.

And that's what keeps me steady: not my strength, but His staying power.

Scripture Reflection:

"I am with you always, to the very end of the age."
—Matthew 28:20

A Prayer of Gratitude for Presence:

God who stays even when I stray,

Thank You for waiting—

Not with judgment,

But with gentleness.

Let me feel You in the pauses,

In the setbacks,

In the days I can't quite pray.

Teach me to stay with others

As You have stayed with me.

Amen.

The Grace That Wouldn't Leave

Charles E. Cravey

I wandered far and slow in shaded doubt,
Where prayers grew thin and praises lost their tune.
Yet grace remained and never called me out,
Just kept a seat beneath forgiveness' moon.

No scolding flame, no sharp rebuke in sight—
Just presence dressed in patience, warm and near.
It held me through my long internal night,
And whispered truth that cast away my fear.

It did not chase me nor demand return,
But let me find my way back through the ache.
And when I did, it did not make me earn—
Just spread out love like biscuits I could take.

So now I know what mercy truly means:
A grace that stays and keeps the porch light clean.

16

"In the Beginning God Rejoiced..."

Where Grace Danced While the Biscuits Rose

B efore sin, before sorrow, before the ache—God rejoiced.

He didn't just make us. He delighted in us. He didn't just provide for us. He celebrated with us. There's something sacred about joy. It's a divine echo of creation's original rhythm.

Mama used to say, "If you can dance while the biscuits rise, you're already halfway to heaven." And I've come to believe that God does just that. Grace is not all solemn candles and bowed heads—it's tambourines and laughter and porch swing confessions that end in hugs.

He rejoices when the prodigal comes home. He rejoices when the faithful keep showing up. He rejoices over the sound of children's giggles and old folks' storytelling.

There's joy in redemption. Joy in restoration. Joy in the daily bread that was prayed for and shared. We often forget that God isn't only holy—He's happy.

His joy isn't dependent on our perfection. It flows from His own nature. He rejoices *because* He is love. And love always celebrates.

If grace has taught me anything, it's that holiness doesn't cancel joy—it invites it to the table.

Scripture Reflection:

"He will rejoice over you with gladness...He will exult over you
with loud singing."
—Zephaniah 3:17

A Prayer of Holy Celebration:

God of joy and dancing,
Thank You for loving me with laughter.
Thank You for being a God
Who sings over the broken,
And plays music for the mended.

Teach me to rejoice not out of duty,
But from delight—
The kind that makes faith feel like freedom.

Amen.

The Grace That Twirls in Morning Light

Charles E. Cravey

He watched me rise from sorrow's quiet place,
And twirled with joy beneath redemption's sun.
No scowl, no scorn, just mercy's warm embrace—
A Father singing, "Welcome home, my son."

The angels laughed, the heavens rang aloud,
Not for perfection, but return made whole.
They danced above the earthly weary crowd,
And stitched rejoicing into every soul.

I once believed God wept more than He smiled,
But grace has shown His laughter leads me on.
His joy is not reserved for just the mild—
It echoes wildly from dusk into dawn.

So let me live beneath that joyful sound,
Where grace rejoices every time I'm found.

17

"In the Beginning God Remembered..."

Where Grace Took Notes in the Margins of My Story

M emory is sacred. Especially divine memory.

God remembers not because He must, but because He chooses to. And when grace remembers, it doesn't just recall—it *honors*. It holds fast to the bruised prayers of our past and brings them forward with blessing.

I've forgotten things. We all have. Birthdays, verses, people who needed one more call. But God? He remembers the seed Mama planted in that Sunday School corner. He remembers the tears that never made it to words. He remembers the promises made at kitchen tables and the hymns hummed half-asleep.

Mama used to say, "God keeps better notes than we do." That gave me peace. Because when my faith falters or my hope runs low, I know grace remembers me—not at my worst, but at my beloved.

The Bible says He remembers His covenant. But I believe He also remembers stories: the moment a child first prayed, the day someone forgave even though they were hurting, the smell of pot roast served in silence to someone grieving.

Grace doesn't forget. It lingers. It keeps records—not to condemn, but to celebrate.

And if grace remembers, then we should too. We remember the saints who showed us mercy. The neighbors who fed us. The strangers who smiled like angels unaware. We write their names in the margins of our stories and offer thanks that God still reads every line.

Scripture Reflection:

"He remembers His covenant forever, the word that He commanded, for a thousand generations."
—Psalm 105:8

A Prayer of Sacred Memory:

God who keeps the stories,
Thank You for remembering
When I forget.

For holding close my broken promises
And turning them into redemption.

Teach me to remember
What others have done in love,
To honor their faithfulness
And pass it along.

Amen.

The Notes That Heaven Still Recalls

Charles E. Cravey

He saw me when the world moved on too fast,
When prayers were whispered yet remained unheard.
He wrote my name upon a sky so vast,
And kept each sigh as if it were a word.

The kindness done in quiet midday hours,
The service missed by all but sacred gaze—
He counted each like petals off a flower,
And stored them deep in mercy's gentle praise.

Though I forget, He never lets slip past
The moments when my heart was turned toward grace.
He stitches them like thread that's made to last,
And paints them into love's eternal space.

So now I live with hope and gratitude—
That I'm remembered, even when I'm subdued.

18

"In the Beginning God Redeemed..."

Where Grace Bought Back What the World Let Go

R edemption is a kind of reclaiming. Not just fixing—but restoring to glory.

God has always been in the business of buying back what the world cast aside. Grace doesn't flinch at brokenness. It leans in, pays the full price, and whispers, "You're worth it."

I've known moments I thought were beyond repair. Decisions I'd like to forget, days I'd rather not remember. But God remembers differently. He doesn't rewind to shame—He rewrites it with mercy.

Mama once said, "God shops the clearance rack and treats it like treasure." That's redemption. It doesn't demand flawlessness—it declares value, even in scars.

The cross itself is a signpost of divine redemption. Not a symbol of defeat, but a celebration of recovery. He didn't just die for sin—He rose for restoration.

I've seen redemption in lives once hardened now tender. In hearts reopened to love. In families stitched back together over grace and gravy and prayer. Redemption isn't a transaction—it's a transformation.

And here's the miracle: God doesn't just redeem what was lost. He makes it better than before. More compassionate. More holy. More useful in the service of love.

When grace redeems, it doesn't just put things back—it sets them free.

Scripture Reflection:

"In Him we have redemption through His blood, the forgiveness of sins, in accordance with the riches of God's grace."
—Ephesians 1:7

A Prayer of Redemption:

God who buys back broken stories,
Thank You for paying the price
Not just to fix me—
But to restore me to purpose.

Let me live like someone redeemed—
Not in pride,
But in grateful wonder.

Make me an agent of redemption
In someone else's life.

Let me speak value
Where the world has spoken failure.

Amen.

The Grace That Paid What I Could Not

Charles E. Cravey

I stood among the ruins of my soul,
The cost too high, the shame too steep to climb.
Yet mercy reached and made the shattered whole,
And marked my life with love outside of time.

No coin I owned could buy back what I'd lost,

No deed erased the weight of all I'd done.

But grace stepped in and bore the final cost,

Not with a word, but through the risen Son.

He didn't flinch at pieces torn apart—

He saw the art within the broken frame.

Redemption breathed into my weary heart,

And called me not by sin, but by my name.

So now I live restored, not second-rate—

A soul rebought by love that conquers fate.

19

"In the Beginning God Sent Me"

Where Grace Wrapped Me in Purpose and Pushed Me Forward

R edemption rarely ends with rest—it blossoms into calling.

God doesn't redeem us to keep us on a shelf. He sends us out like letters written in love and sealed with purpose. And Grace? Grace is the stamp that says, "This one is ready."

I've felt that holy nudge in moments I didn't expect. A friend who needed listening more than advice. A community that didn't know it was hungering for hope. A Sunday school class that showed me faith wasn't taught—it was shared like cornbread and stories.

My grandmother once said, "When grace changes you, it doesn't let you sit long. It hands you a casserole and sends you across the street." That's how God sends us—into places that need warmth, presence, and love. Not grand stages, but porch steps and open doors.

God sends us not because we are perfect but because we are willing. Grace equips. Grace emboldens. Grace transforms fear into readiness. I've been sent into grief, into celebration, and into quiet discipleship. Each time, Grace paved the way.

We are messengers in clay shoes, delivering letters written in mercy and signed by Heaven. That's a job worth showing up for.

Scripture Reflection:

"As the Father has sent Me, I also send you."
—John 20:21

A Prayer of Willingness:

God, who sends and sustains,

I may not feel qualified—

But I am willing.

Let me carry Your message

Into living rooms,

Into grocery aisles,

Into hearts starved for hope.

Send me with grace,

And let me return with stories

Of Your faithfulness.

Amen.

The Path That Opened When Grace Said "Go"

Charles E. Cravey

I stood restored, unsure of what came next,
But Grace reached out and placed the call in hand.
Not by decree, not by a scroll of text,
But through a stillness I could understand.

He did not send me far from where I stand—
Just close enough to see another's pain.
He used my scars to meet their own demand,
And turned my steps into a holy lane.

I do not travel with a prophet's voice,
But with a heart that's touched by Heaven's fire.
He sends the humble—not the loudest choice—
To be a balm, a bridge, a quiet choir.

So now I walk with purpose not my own—
Sent by the One whose love has always known.

20

"In the Beginning God Welcomed Me..."

Where Grace Flung Open the Door Before I Knocked

G od's welcome is never reluctant.

He doesn't peek through the curtain to decide if we're clean enough. He throws open the door and says, *"You're right on time."* It's grace that greets us barefoot, arms wide, apron still on, table set for more than expected.

I've felt that welcome in church pews, hospital rooms, porch swings, and casseroles. In letters I didn't know I needed. In forgiveness I hadn't earned. In laughter that returned after a long absence.

Mama once told me, "We set an extra plate even if we're not expecting anyone—because grace always expects someone." That's how God welcomes. Not with caution, but with celebration.

He welcomed the prodigal. He welcomed the thief on the cross. He welcomes us—not as guests, but as family. Grace removes the velvet rope and says, *"Come on in. No one's too late."*

And once we're welcomed, we're changed. Not because we were forced to be—but because being loved that well rewrites us.

The miracle is this: God doesn't just welcome us once. He keeps welcoming. Every time we wander. Every time we return. Every time we whisper, "I didn't know if I could come back."

He replies, "You never left My heart."

Scripture Reflection:

"Come to Me, all you who are weary and burdened, and I will give you rest."
—Matthew 11:28

A Prayer of Arrival:

God who leaves the light on,
Thank You for making room
Before I knew I'd need it.

Thank You for calling me "beloved",
Before I ever called You "Lord."

Teach me to welcome others
As You have welcomed me—
With warmth,
With joy,
With zero hesitation.

Amen.

The Door That Never Locked

Charles E. Cravey

I stumbled in, unsure if I belonged.
My soul still sore from roads that bent and broke.
Yet grace arose like morning's simplest song,
And met me with embrace, not scorn or yoke.

No questions asked, no ledger brought to bear,
Just open arms and table filled with light.
He saw the weary shadow in my stare,
And answered it with hospitality's might.

I stayed not out of fear, but love grown deep—
A welcome not withdrawn with passing time.
It taught me grace is more than promises we keep—
It's doors that open wide and bells that chime.

So now I live with arms forever spread,
Welcoming others just as I was led.

Epilogue: Mama Always Knew

A Quiet Goodbye and a Lasting Welcome

B aby, if you're holding this book, you've already sat at the table.

You've tasted the grace stirred into these pages, the kind that doesn't just fill your belly—it fills your soul. And maybe—just maybe—it's reminded you that God's never been far. Not in the noise. Not in the mess. Not even in the forgetting. He's been there. Spoon in hand. Light on. Apron tied.

You see, I always believed that grace was like gravy—you start with what's left over. What the world might overlook. Then you stir in faith, a little heat, and a lotta love. And what you get is enough. More than enough.

I watched your life, Charles. Watched your heart stretch wide and your prayers fly higher than the clothesline. I knew God had His hand on you before you knew what prayer even sounded like. And I watched Grace chase you down every chapter—through joy, through tears, through every potluck of purpose.

So here we are. The book's written. The table's been set. But the story? Honey, it's still going.

This isn't goodbye—it's "save me a seat."

Keep writing. Keep stirring. Keep welcoming folks into the kitchen of your life.

Because Grace isn't finished.

And neither are you.

Love always,

Mama (In Memory of Irene Cooper Cravey—"Rest in Peace")

About the Author

Charles E. Cravey is a storyteller, a servant, and a soul-stirrer whose words carry the warmth of Sunday suppers and the reverence of sacred scripture. With over five decades of love woven into his marriage, faith journey, and creative life, Charles writes not merely to be heard but to be felt. His devotionals and faith-centered books brim with spiritual depth, Southern hospitality, and a quiet invitation to live slowly, love deeply, and walk humbly.

Through works like *Biscuits and Grace* and *Grace and Gravy*, Charles cultivates spaces of comfort and clarity—where readers find nourishment for both body and spirit. His chapters echo the wisdom of Mama, the truths of scripture, and the everyday miracles tucked into casseroles, porches, and pews.

Charles believes in community, calling, and the enduring beauty of grace passed down across generations. His writing honors the quiet heroes, the tender prayers, and the lives made sacred by kindness.

He lives, writes, and welcomes—one story at a time.

The Rev. Dr. Roger Songster, Brighton, England

OTHER BOOKS BY DR. CRAVEY MAY BE FOUND AT:

https://drcharlescravey.com OR

Amazon.com/Charles Cravey Books

www.ingramcontent.com/pod-product-compliance
Lightning Source LLC
LaVergne TN
LVHW011208080426
835508LV00007B/663